Ducks

DUCKS

Art, Legend, History

Anna Giorgetti

Series editor: Giorgio Coppin

The Bulfinch Library of Collectibles

A Bulfinch Press Book
Little, Brown and Company
Boston · Toronto · London

First North American Edition

English translation by Helena Ramsay
Series editor: Giorgio Coppin

Library of Congress Cataloging-in-Publication Data

Giorgetti, Anna.
   [Anatre & papere. English]
   Ducks: art, legend, history/Anna Giorgetti.—1st North American ed.
      p.   cm. —(The Bulfinch library of collectibles)
   "A Bulfinch Press book."
   ISBN 0-8212-2010-1
   1. Ducks—Collectibles.   2. Ducks—Legends.   3. Ducks—History.
   I. Title. II. Series.
   NK4898.5.O5613   1992
   704.9'432—dc20
                                          92-30854

Bulfinch Press is an imprint and trademark of Little, Brown and Company (Inc.)
Published simultaneously in Canada by Little, Brown & Company (Canada) Limited

PRINTED IN ITALY

CONTENTS

In Sanskrit, geese, ducks and swans were all referred to as hansa *or sacred water birds. The family group is shown here on top of an English table decorated with a wild duck carving. A splendid English tea cosy in the form of a mallard, an Italian goose teapot and a small silver gosling tea caddy make up the tea service. The only family member missing is the swan.*

A great family

So where exactly do the ducks in Central Park go when the lake freezes over? This question troubled Holden, the hero of J. D. Salinger's famous novel *The Catcher in the Rye*. While we may not share his deep concern for the ducks of Central Park, we may often ask ourselves similar questions about their wilder counterparts as they pass overhead each year. We know that they always try to winter somewhere with a mild climate and plenty of food. We can also imagine that they set off hoping they will not meet with too much trouble from hunters on the way. So far so good, but how on earth do they manage to pack their bags, gather their families and fly off in that classic "V" formation on time, at the same time, each year? We stand there, noses in the air, praying that the squadron leader will take care, not run risks, stay on course and lead the whole flight to safety. But then it is daft to worry really, as they never do make any mistakes, and those of us who have very little sense of direction can only be filled with admiration and envy when we consider their ability.

Of course, we are not just talking about ducks here. There are geese, swans and all the other aquatic birds that share the same fortune in being able to float on water as well as soar through the air at will.

All of these birds belong to the Anatidae family – a word derived from the Latin verb *anas*, to swim. They share many physical features such as webbed feet, short legs and long necks. Broadly speaking, the different species also have similar beaks with horny lamellae or plates which serve as filters and are indispensable during feeding.

All the members of this family are strong flyers. It is easy to distinguish them from other birds in flight on account of their rapid wing beats and long, out-stretched necks which contrast curiously with their almost truncated bodies. As well as being fine flyers they are also strong swimmers. All of them can survive happily in the most inhospitable conditions – hence the expression "nice weather for ducks."

This duck is hewn from Swedish crystal and has the luminous quality of a primitive, symbolic creature. The china couple on the opposite page were made in Faenza, Italy. They are a picture of conjugal fidelity – a quality traditionally symbolized by the duck.

"Like water off a duck's back" is also a popular expression, used to describe something that has no effect. It is derived from another interesting family characteristic: ducks, geese and swans have completely waterproof plumage on account of the constant secretion of oil from their uropygium glands. As a result water runs off them instantly and they are comfortable in water for unlimited lengths of time. Ducklings and goslings take to the water within a few hours of hatching. With their webbed feet and their wide bodies they soon become strong and talented swimmers, able to resist both wind and waves.

Fine flying is of course the other speciality of this family. Wild geese of the family Anserinae (from *anser* or goose in Latin) certainly take the first prize in this field. As a professed goose lover, what would I not give to swap places with a pilot when his flight path is crossed by wild geese at more than ten thousand feet?

Birds have evolved relatively slowly in comparison to other animals. Fossilized remains show that ducks and geese already existed in virtually their present form during the

Cenozoic era, between fifty and one hundred million years ago. Nobody knows whether they were as beautiful then as they are now. It may have taken centuries to achieve the breathtaking beauty of the ducks, swans and geese that share our affections today.

Over the centuries the physical similarities between the three cousins has led them to take interchangeable roles in the myths and legends of popular culture. However, this tendency to swap ducks for geese and vice versa may also be due to the derivation of their names. The German word *Gans* and the English *goose* derive from *anser* or *hanser* in Latin. This in turn corresponds to the Sanskrit *hansa* (sometimes rendered as *hamsa* or *hangsa*). In Sanskrit the word was used indifferently to mean swan, duck, goose and even flamingo.

Below: a carving made in Thailand in the 1940s. Opposite: a papier-mâché duck from Venice. On the preceding pages: a pair of Belgian mandarin ducks in red and black with fine detail in gold.

In Russian fairy tales the baby hero or heroine is often saved by a swan–goose. The sacred texts of the Brahmins also feature duck–swans and geese–swans in important roles. Agni, god of fire, is compared to a flaming *hansa* on the water. By extension, the mythical bird is then compared to a star in the sky like a glowing fountain in the shadows. The *hansa* is often linked to precious stones and metals. In the Rig-Veda, the most ancient of the Indian religious texts, there are ducks that lay golden eggs in a nest built, curiously enough, on the head of a thief. Sometimes the bird is linked to Indra himself, the warrior god, guardian of social and cosmic order.

Afanasyev's Russian fairy tales include the story of two servants who steal a precious pearl from their master the king. They are about to be found out when they manage to disguise the pearl as a lump of lard and feed it to a grey goose. They then shift the blame from their own heads by accusing the goose of theft. The king has the goose slaughtered and recovers the pearl. The true thieves are never punished and the story serves to highlight the cruel tricks that man has always played on animals, both in fact and fable.

This brass duck–goose looks a little dazed. He may well have just landed after an arduous flight, perhaps thousands of miles long.

Wildfowl have other roles to play in Indian mythology. Brahma himself is portrayed on the back of a white *hansa*. In the Ramayana the sky is compared to a great lake and the sun to a beautiful golden duck.

To continue on the subject of lakes and ducks that may or may not be golden, there is another episode among Afanasyev's tales. A father tells his son to seek a wife who he will find in the shape of a duck. His instructions are somewhat enigmatic: "Go to Moscow," he says, "there you will find a lake and in the lake there will be a net. If there is a duck in the net put your hand on it, otherwise pull the net in." A few, but obviously vital words of advice – and we all know what trouble a father will take to marry off his son! Needless to say, the son comes home with his duck, or rather, his wife.

This Chinese duck is modelled in painted stone. Judging by its colourful plumage, it must be a drake. Such an attire is ideal for catching the eye of a female.

In the Ramayana, Rama himself shoots an arrow from his divine bow. It flies over seven palms, a mountain and the earth itself before returning to the god in the form of a *hansa*.

Hansa appear yet again in the Mahabharata, one of the great epic poems of ancient India, where Prince Nala and Princess Damayanti use them as messengers.

Moving once again from India to Russia, our next hero is little Ivan, stolen by geese–swans while his sister, who should have been looking after him, is distracted. Ivan is then carried to the house of a fairy where, amongst other things, he plays with some apples made of gold. Altogether, it is quite an adventure for a little boy! The story makes the point, however, that these birds were once believed to catch and eat little children. In fact, a lengthy part of the story is

dedicated to the guilty sister's desperate search for her brother. In the end she finds him and, heaving a sigh of relief, she carries him home. Unfortunately, on the way she is pursued by the goose–swans and only just manages to escape.

In notes to this fairy tale we learn that ducks, geese and swans, so *hansa* in general, are only occasionally used in this way to portray evil or the devil himself. It is much more common to find the *hansa* represented as a positive force of goodness. Knowing this then, as admirers of the *hansa*, perhaps we can explain their role in the story of Ivan. Obviously little Ivan was happy to collude with the birds which actually proved to be his friends for, naturally, he was thrilled to go with the geese–swans to the fairy's house where he could play with the golden apples away from his irritating sister.

A particularly loving and gentle mother is sometimes referred to as a "mother goose." Geese are in fact very protective towards their young, as this Italian carving in balsa wood shows.

With their endearingly plump bodies, their clumsy gait and their heads in continuous movement as they swim vigorously along in front of their families, it is certainly difficult to imagine ducks as anything but benign creatures. Yet, both ducks and geese can be quite aggressive and appearances, as we all know, can be deceptive.

It is actually the gender of the species that is distinguished by physical aspects. Like so many of the "stronger sex" in the animal kingdom, the male has to make himself noticed by the females. This feature, which is common among all birds, is particularly pronounced in the Anatidae family. In fact, in most species the males and females have quite different plumage; the common goose is the only well known exception to this rule. The brightly coloured plumage of the males acts as a signal to the opposite sex and particular movements of the body and feathers are made to accentuate the effect. Females usually have simple plumage with subdued colours such as brown and grey. These colours also serve a purpose, for during the nesting period they act as an effective camouflage to protect the birds from predators. For the rest of the year the males and females look very similar then, shortly before the mating season, the drake's appearance is transformed by a new, rich nuptial plumage.

While the metallic green feathers on the shoveler, the chestnut teal and many of the mergansers, and the orange head of the red-crested duck are very striking, it is not only colour that makes the new plumage so splendid and attractive to mates. The drakes of many species also alter the form and arrangement of the feathers. Many mandarin ducks and some mergansers develop striking crests, while

This candle in the shape of a duck recalls the Indian myth in which the duck is compared to a star shining out of the darkness. Opposite: this duck–swan was made in 1910 and comes from Madras in Southern India.

maned and Orinoco geese produce a new collar for the mating season. Many species of wildfowl develop a type of mirror on the upperwing. This is made up of a series of feathers that are almost metallic in colour. When the birds are in flight they use the "mirrors" on each other's wings as a form of optical signalling device that helps them to stay together and in formation. It is this variety of form and colour in the water birds' feathers that makes them a true joy to behold.

The sounds made by male and female ducks differ considerably, while the call of the male and female swan or goose is much the same. All birds use their calls as a form of communication. Sometimes the calls serve as a warning to others not to enter their territory, sometimes as an alarm call and sometimes as a means of maintaining contact whilst in flight. Aquatic birds have a far more limited range of sounds. These are used to warn of danger and also as contact calls to reassure and warn their babies when they stray too far from the nest. Calls used during night flights are also vitally important. Clearly, these too are a means of keeping the flight in formation and ensuring that nobody is lost. Both the duck and the drake of the mallard species let out a high pitched call to each other. Although the calls are very loud, they actually serve as a form of mutual reassurance. To an observer, the couple sound like a husband and wife having a momentary violent row. Then, having shouted and sworn at each other, they return, as if nothing had happened, to a mutual preening session.

While on the subject of sound signals, we must turn our minds for a moment to the renowned ethologist, Konrad Lorenz. Like any good foster parent, he learned to communicate with his innumerable children. He tells an enchanting tale of his first night with Martina, the little grey goose. Once Martina had accepted Lorenz as her mother, she would not leave his side for an instant. She would call to him regularly throughout the night, like any other baby in need of reassurance. It is not difficult to imagine how the scientist felt about these constant interruptions to his sleep.

A Danish goose carved from wood. Its combative stance is characteristic – geese have been used as watchdogs ever since they guarded Campidoglio, seat of the Roman Empire, against the Gauls. They are still used in this way on American farms today.

Finally, however, he came up with a solution. The moment Martina began her characteristic "lost piping" call (an emergency signal meaning "Here I am – where are you?"), Lorenz would respond with the appropriate "contact" call, like any other mother goose. The gosling settled down at once. Gradually, Lorenz found himself able to respond in his sleep to her urgent cries for attention. He believed that from then on he would always be able to come up with the appropriate response to anyone uttering the lost piping to him while he slept! And who are we to argue?

Aquatic birds, or *hansa*, do not rely on sound alone. They also use movement as a means of communication. The mating ritual, for example, resembles a true minuet, danced with rigorous steps and timings. To begin with, couples do not meet by accident in isolation; the whole process takes place at what might resemble a huge singles party. A male and a female swim together and then drink at the same moment, showing with these precise signals that they have abandoned any trace of hostility. The male then becomes agitated, stretches out his neck, shakes his head vigorously and holds his neck over his chosen partner. The female, in her turn, watches the gander closely, shakes her head and calls, inviting him to protect her from other suitors. There is little real need for his protection, for by this time matters are virtually concluded between them. However, in the game of love, as we all know, it never does to be too confident and many a human has played the same game.

Among geese and swans the males and females have their own rituals in courtship. They face each other, rub the tops of their heads together, ruffle their feathers and turn their heads from side to side. Among ducks, however, it is

the drakes that take the more active role. The duck appears to be quite indifferent to the drake as he shakes his head, preens his feathers and, depending on species, shows her either his head or his tail. This exhibition continues until she adopts a flat posture on the water and accepts him.

After swans have mated, they go to the edge of the water, stretch their necks, shake their heads and let out great cries, which possibly signal mutual satisfaction. Geese cry out too, the gander stretching his neck and wings as he does so. Ducks, on the other hand, swim gracefully away from one another. We can only presume that these are all signs of heartfelt passion. Perhaps the most romantic bird of all is the red-crested duck, the drake of which presents the duck of his choice with a leaf or two before mating. The effect is similar to that of a young man with a bunch of red roses for the girl of his dreams on their first date. And how many of us would not wish our nearest and dearest to take a lesson from the red-crested duck?

Below: a little Polish duck made from painted wood. Perhaps it is a descendant of the geese–swans of Russian fairy tales who kidnap or save the life of the young hero, depending on the tale. Opposite: a wooden duck from Africa inlaid with brass. The wings are carved from bone. One species, the pintail, flies all the way from central Russia to Senegal to pass the winter.

Waddling like a duck

It is true. On dry land our friend the duck could not be described as a paragon of grace or agility. With that rolling gait and the webbed feet sticking out to either side they are hardly likely to attract admiring glances.

So what excuse can we find them. We could compare them to a ballerina, for example. Have you ever noticed how ballerinas walk when they have a break from the stage or the practice bar and mix with us mortals? We may see them in the street doing their shopping or catching a bus like anyone else. And what do they look like? They too walk with their feet sticking out, so even their movements could scarcely be described as graceful. The fact is we only have to look at a duck or a goose to understand their true potential. They have long, flexible necks, straight, supple spines and muscular legs. Just as a ballerina is out of place in the supermarket or the post office, nearly all waterfowl are out of their element on dry land. Dancers and ducks are made for particular habitats. When we watch an ethereal ballerina spring into the air as if oblivious to the force of

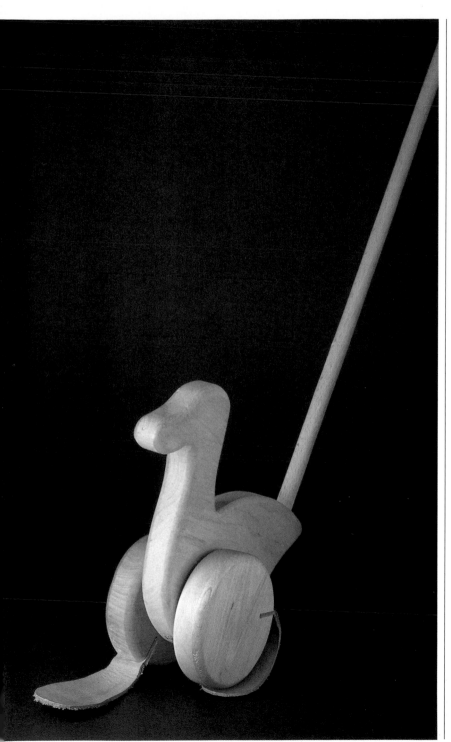

gravity, we forget the fleeting glimpse that we had of her as a clumsy figure behind a trolley full of shopping. In the same way, when we see our *hansa* sporting in the water or flying with perfect grace and vigour through the sky, we never pause to consider how clumsy they look walking along the river bank.

The torrent duck is a particularly fine swimmer. It is very slim and has a beautiful cherry-red beak. It lives on the raging torrents of the Andes at anything up to 11,500 feet (3,600 m). It has an incredible aptitude for going over rapids in descent and, amazingly enough, in ascent as well. It launches itself with apparent indifference into the waves, showing no anxiety about the sharp rocks or the strong current. It can sometimes be seen nonchalantly climbing across waterfalls. It is true that these skills only show themselves when the duck is escaping from danger, but would we ever throw ourselves voluntarily into the rapids? We might try to survive if we were thrown in, but our chances of success would be few.

Diving ducks have squat bodies and very large feet. Their wings are short and pointed. In order to take off they have to run along the surface of the water, flapping their wings frantically. Once they are airborne, however, they are extremely able flyers. Nevertheless, as their name suggests, their true speciality is staying under the water rather than above it. Some species are able to go down as far as 160 feet (50 m).

There are tales of wounded ducks that have escaped the shoot by hiding under water with only their eyes and beaks showing. Others are said to swim to the bottom, hold on to a bit of weed with their feet and die there rather than being shot. To romantics it may seem that they prefer suicide to capture by the enemy. In reality, however, it is simply a desperate but misjudged attempt to escape.

Our friend the duck is a truly polyvalent creature, a master of three elements: earth, water and air. It is hardly surprising then that it should occupy such an important place in our imagination.

Below: a beautiful Italian porcelain mallard that displays all the strength of the bird's character. Opposite: this duck has a more peaceful air to it but this is probably deceptive since it is really a little clockwork duck, made in Taiwan.

Traditionally, in theories on the origins and development of the earth, water has been seen as the source of life, a means of purification and regeneration, a symbol of fecundity and fertility. According to Indian legend, the world was born out of a cosmic egg, the "Brahmanda." Birds, we know, all lay eggs, but the Brahmanda was laid at the waters' edge and so it goes without saying that it must have been laid by a *hansa!*

Water is seen as the source of creation by Jews and Christians alike. Its role, however, is ambivalent. It brings life and death; it is both a creator and a destroyer. Hesiod expounds the symbolic differences between fresh and salt water. Fresh, still water is drawn from a pool or a lake and it symbolizes woman. Foaming salt water is from the sea and it symbolizes man. Perhaps it is because the duck is associated with the still waters of the pool or lake that it has often been depicted as having a more female nature.

Once in the water *hansa* are without a care in the world. They pass the time looking for food and they amuse themselves by keeping on the move and making sudden, unexpected and rapid dives. After studying his wild geese, Konrad Lorenz defined this as diving for fun. The goose dives, comes up, swims along the surface for a while and then, quite suddenly, dives again. As he moves along he will abruptly and continuously change direction for no apparent reason. According to Lorenz this is most likely to be a means of defense against airborne predators, so fun is really an inappropriate word to describe these activities that are prompted by anything but playful impulses.

At less than two inches high this English goose is surprisingly heavy, being made out of cast iron. She has every right to be so proud of her egg as, according to Indian mythology, the world itself originated from an egg.

The duck is an aquatic bird, which means that it can fly and swim. During migration it flies at considerable altitudes, crossing seas and continents. Only other migrating birds are so fortunate and almost every other creature on this earth accepts that the vaulted heavens are beyond its reach. Man, however, is an exception. With his insatiable desire to explore and to conquer new horizons, he has defied nature and travelled to the farthest reaches of the skies in an attempt to share the freedom that birds have shown him. He has paid dearly for his achievements over the decades.

This Spanish duck is painted in almost muted tones. Water is a duck's natural element and their plumage is especially adapted to be particularly waterproof.

Nevertheless, despite the risks and the disappointments, envy and fascination has spurred him on. Every failure has been followed by a return to the drawing board and the invention of a new solution.

Conquering the skies does not simply mean moving about in them and possessing them in the physical sense. In almost every cultural tradition the sky symbolizes all that is sacred, powerful and eternal. In symbolic terms the conquest of the skies raises man to a transcendental position, giving him power and dominion over all of his

*The shape of this fine wooden duck is
identical to that of the classic decoy ducks
used by hunters. It comes from Texas and
was decorated by hand using paint and
poker-work.*

surroundings. In ancient times the Celts, Greeks, Egyptians,
Hindus and Chinese all believed that the sky was the upper
half of the cosmic egg. And it is here that ducks and geese
can reside as well as on the ground and in water. Up there,
where the spirit achieves perfection, they fly about, lords of
the air, caring nothing for airstrips or landing pads. Some of
them, like helicopters, can even rise vertically into the air
from a standstill.

Martina, who was Lorenz's first wild goose, showed
remarkable aviation skills even before her wing feathers

Another clockwork toy made out of tin in Taiwan. It gives a fine impression of the waterfowls' extraordinary abilities in flight. They can actually reach an altitude of 33,000 feet (10,000 m) and a speed of 60 miles (100 km) per hour.

were properly developed. One day Lorenz and Martina were coming home after a walk. Progress was rather slow as the young goose was not one for stepping out vigorously. Eventually Lorenz became impatient. He made flying signals to Martina (signals that were probably unknown to anyone but him and the goose) and then ran off towards home. She started to follow him and soon took off, flying faster and higher by the minute. She flew right across a field towards a line of fir trees. By the time she noticed them it was too late to slow down. Rather than crashing into the trees, however, she was able to pull up and rise high above them, soon disappearing beyond. Lorenz searched everywhere for Martina before going back to the house. He knew that the area beyond the trees was mountainous terrain, full of every kind of difficulty for a junior flyer. He returned home resigned to the idea that the gosling was lost for ever. There, to his amazement, he found Martina curled up on the doormat. The absence of her foster mother had made her very anxious, but when Lorenz arrived she was soon her normal self again and gave him a raucous welcome. Martina must have overcome numerous physical difficulties on her return journey. More remarkable still was the ability to find her way at all. She had never been that way before so she must have relied on an extraordinary sense of direction. This instinctive skill, a trait shared with many bird families, is essential during migration.

The majority of swans and geese leave the Arctic Circle in winter for Holland, Great Britain and France. Some white-fronted geese fly directly from Greenland to northwest Scotland and Ireland without stopping. Others stop off for a week or two in Iceland. The distance between their breeding grounds in Greenland and the places

where they winter is at least 2,000 miles (3,500 km). Some species of duck make even longer journeys. Pintails migrate from central Russia to Senegal. Pochards and wigeons regularly undertake journeys in excess of 3,000 miles (5,000 km). How do migrating birds make such arduous flights without ever losing their way? There are various theories involving the use of the moon, the sun and the stars for navigation. Some people even suggest that their sense of direction is linked in some way to the earth's magnetic field. In general, birds use physical features such as shorelines, watercourses, valleys and passes. Whatever the system, their progress is swift and accurate. Swans and geese fly at between 45 and 50 miles (70 and 80 km) per hour. Some breeds of duck reach 68 miles (110 km) per hour, and with favourable winds they can even reach 100 miles (160 km) per hour. The white-fronted goose's non-stop 2,000-mile (3,500-km) journey from Greenland probably takes about 48 hours.

Most aquatic birds settle down to nest in the same area each year. This is not a question of instinct alone. Swans, geese and, to a lesser extent, ducks are good teachers. They make sure that their young become familiar with their winter quarters and that they know exactly where it is. The information is not, therefore, genetically acquired but is

Below: a soft and colourful cuddly toy created in France. The duck opposite, on the other hand, arouses a sense of awe. It is carved from a splendid opal. Perhaps it is the incarnation of Seb, the Ancient Egyptian god of the earth.

imparted to each new generation by the parents. This fact was demonstrated by various experiments carried out on geese. Geese raised in captivity were incapable of finding their way to traditional breeding grounds. It was only after they were introduced into a group of wild geese that they began to learn where to go.

Wildfowl are intensely gregarious creatures. During migration families and larger groups stay together. They identify each other and communicate along strictly hierarchical lines. Even a bird without any family would never dream of migrating alone. Despite its isolation it will always migrate with the rest of the flock.

The mysterious "V" formation made by geese and ducks

A family of wooden Polish ducks. Parents and elders teach their young the route to their winter quarters, for geese and ducks do not travel by instinct; they have to be taught how to do it.

in flight has always been a cause for curiosity. The theory is that it is a means of producing maximum results for the minimum expenditure of energy by each individual bird. Every member of the flock is helped along by the rising currents produced by the wing beats of the bird in front. This system also operates in the water. Ducks and geese never swim in a long line. Each one swims next to the wake of the one in front, keeping just far enough away from the preceding bird to have a clear view of the path ahead. Similarly, when they are about to take off they arrange their positions just enough to give each an unimpaired view. Once airborne and in formation each bird has such an extensive view that it can see all the other birds in the group. This means that they can all see the signals given by the bird at the apex of the triangle. The leading bird is not always the "captain" of the group. Responsibility for leadership is shared among a number of different birds and it is vital that the leaders should be visible to every member of the flock.

This flight formation, especially during migration, acts as a means of preservation and as such serves indirectly to ensure the survival of the species. During migration the group behaves rather like a foreign legion. The well-being of one member counts for nothing as the group is of paramount importance, so weak or sickly birds inevitably succumb and the others will do nothing to save them. The group takes its orders from a few individuals. Nobody knows exactly how the leaders are selected but they are probably the oldest and most experienced birds in the flock. They are certainly the most skilled. Migration is a collective phenomenon, a mass movement involving the individual in something greater than himself. It may be that it does not

37

exactly coincide with his own desires and objectives, but this is irrelevant. He is no longer an individual in his own right but a part of the whole. Continuous reciprocal communication allows each individual to preserve his own position which, in turn, maintains the order of the entire group. This arrangement means the flight is a fluid and unified mass composed of individuals devoted to the collective good.

Migration represents one particular aspect of the flying skills of some species of bird. When in flight, however, every bird becomes a symbol of the relationship between the earth and the sky. In some traditions the soul itself is seen as a bird. In ancient Indian texts the soul is always portrayed as a web-footed bird, the *hansa*, in fact, that we have already discussed. According to the theory of reincarnation, the soul travels from body to body until, finally, it flies to the nest of the *hansa* where it seeks refuge from further, unwanted reincarnations.

Both of these ducks are made out of wood.
The one above is a jewellery box from
Eastern Europe; opposite: an abacus made
in the People's Republic of China. The
endearing little family on the previous pages
comes from Uruguay. They are made out of
terracotta.

The duck's superiority over other birds, however, lies in
the fact that it is aquatic which means that it not only knows
how to fly, but can swim as well! This is why it has attracted
mankind's envy and become a symbol in his dreams, a
subject for his fantasies. Imagine the psychoanalyst whose
patient tells him that he has dreamt about a duck. How will
the poor doctor know which of our friend's three
dimensions to concentrate on. Will it be earth, air or water?

These three aspects of the duck's nature have a symbolic
force that always arouses contradictory emotions in us.
They have all our admiration when they fly or swim. This
absolute dominion spans the elements normally inhabited
by two completely different species: birds and fish. It is not
surprising that as poor, earthbound bipeds we should feel in
awe. When, on the other hand, they waddle about with that
air of uncertainty, ducks arouse the tenderest feelings in us.
They simply become sweet little feathered creatures to be
protected. All revered totem-animals are, in fact, protective
spirits while, in turn, they are protected by man. Man may
kill them to eat the flesh and use the feathers and skins, but

then as way of compensation he sings their praises and celebrates festivals in their honour. Additionally, he ensures that they thrive and proliferate. He should be a thoughtful hunter and not kill indiscriminately. He carrys out fertility dances so that the birds will reproduce abundantly. After the dancing the hunting can begin. Life is invoked so that death may follow. It is all a bizarre repetitive circle in our relationship with nature.

Traditionally, Native Americans were masters of the symbiotic and magical relationship between man and nature. They worshipped the three elements and all the creatures within them. Their sustenance was drawn entirely from air, earth and water. Living in harmony with nature, they were the antithesis of man in the technological age.

Anyone who enjoys ancient stories will be interested in the Native American tales about the origins of the horse. The Navaho and the Apaches believed that the sun moulded horses from coloured clay and then let them roam freely on the earth. According to other tribes, such as the Shoshone and the Blackfoot, the horse was originally an aquatic animal. In the Blackfoot tale a young orphan boy

stood crying one day on the river bank. He was alone in the world and did not know where to turn. The spirit of the water, a wise old man who lived at the bottom of the lake, heard his sobs. He sent his son to find the boy and ask him why he was crying. When he found the boy, the son of the spirit of the water took him on his shoulders and descended to the depths. On the way he gave him some advice: "My father will offer you any one of the animals that live in the lake. Remember to choose the oldest duck and all of her babies." Everything was as the son had predicted. The kind old spirit offered the boy a gift to make up for his misfortunes. "I would be very grateful if you could give me the oldest duck and her young," said the boy. "You don't want her," the spirit replied, "she is old and worthless." The boy insisted. He asked four times for the duck and

These beautiful wild ducks are made out of porcelain and come from Copenhagen. They could be asleep, or perhaps they are preening themselves. According to Plautus, the Latin playwright, ducks preen when the wind is about to increase.

finally the old man smiled and said: "You are a wise young man. When it gets dark you can leave, taking the duck with you. Tie a cord around her neck and don't look back until sunrise." On dry land again, the boy set off into the darkness towards his camp. As he walked he heard the duck's feathers beating on the ground. Suddenly the sound changed and he heard heavy footsteps behind him. Then, every now and then there was the cry of an animal that he had never heard before. At last dawn broke and the boy looked behind him. There was no longer a duck with her young on the end of his rope but a procession of strange creatures that he had never seen before. They were horses. When he got home his tribe were frightened of the strange animals. Gradually, however, they gained confidence. They learned to ride them and use them for carrying loads and hunting bison. One day the men of the tribe asked "Would these animals be useful in water?" "Of course," said the boy, "for that is where they came from." Then he showed

them how to use the horses for crossing streams and rivers.

When he grew up the boy was elected chief of the tribe. From that day forth every Blackfoot chief has had numerous horses.

Native Americans discovered the horse relatively recently. In most places, the first time they saw a horse it carried a white man on its back. Naturally, they initially thought that the strange creature must be the mother of the being that it carried on its back. This leads us on to another theory: if some Native Americans thought that the horse was the man's mother, and the horse was said to be descended from the duck, can we not presume, then, that the duck was the progenitor of mankind? It is another attractive hypothesis, but nothing more. Led on by our love for the duck, perhaps we have been a little too imaginative.

What could be more symbolic for an aquatic bird than being transformed into a jug? The one below is from Vienna and dates from the 1940s. The original creation opposite is a table decoration or perhaps an egg basket. It is made out of porcelain and comes from Italy.

As clever as a goose

It is all too easy to call somebody a "silly old goose" and yet it is a foolish thing to say. And have you noticed how it is always women who are referred to as "geese" or "ducky"? You will never hear a man being called a "silly gosling," and this in any language. To qualify as a silly goose all you need do is to be happy and contented instead of suffering in silence, pining away or otherwise dramatizing the evils of this world. Some people do not understand how much easier it is to take life seriously and how infinitely more difficult — and consequently more commendable — it is to be humorous about it. Ducks and geese appear to have just this attitude. They flutter here and there, happily waddling about on their great big feet. They are loving and tender mothers, but aggressive if their young are threatened. They show enormous courage when the need arises and they will even attack humans.

Most people have heard the tale about the geese on the Capitoline Hill in Rome. In A.D. 387, it was their brave

defense that saved the city from the Barbarians. Geese were sacred to Juno and this meant that they were linked with marriage and fertility. At the same time their intervention during the Barbarian attack on the Capitol tied them to Mars, god of war. To this day they are such good guardians that some farms in America use them in place of dogs.

In Egypt and China wild geese were depicted as messengers between the sky and the earth. In Egypt the Pharaoh was identified with the sun and his soul was represented by a goose. This was because both the sun and the goose came out of the primordial egg. The advent of a new Pharaoh was marked by many rituals including one in which four wild ducks were thrown towards the four separate corners of the horizon. One of them was ordered to "Hurry South and tell the kings of the South that a new Pharaoh has been crowned." The others were sent to the North, East and West with the same instructions.

Legend has it that Seb, the Egyptian god of the earth, took the form of a goose, his sacred animal. Paintings of geese and ducks have been found on numerous Egyptian tombs and mausoleums. Sometimes they are shown as wild birds to be hunted and sometimes as semi-domestic creatures in cages. Other paintings show geese and ducks being tended in a flock. Even these, however, may not have been entirely domesticated.

Ducks were certainly domesticated later than geese and were then seen as purely ornamental creatures. They often appear in idyllic scenes showing gardens, lakes and groups of nobles busy eating dates in the shade of a palm tree. In the ancient world the duck was of greater importance to the hunter than the farmer. It did not appear on the Nile until the twelfth dynasty and it was unknown to the Hebrews. Equally the Greeks and the Italic peoples only occasionally raised ducks.

The establishment of the duck as a domestic animal in Europe may have something to do with the cult of Aphrodite. On the islands of Rhodes and Cyprus, famous for the worship of Venus, ancient vases in the shape of ducks have been discovered. Sometimes they depict Aphrodite riding the duck and sometimes they are simply

Below: this wooden duck was made in India in the 1920s. Opposite: a wooden paper clip decorated with marbled paper. It holds an envelope with American stamps dating from 1968. An Indian printing block lies on top of the envelope.

This modern sauce boat in the shape of a duck was made in France. Opposite: a bakelite duck brush made in the 1940s in England. There are, as you can see, ducks and geese to suit every purpose and taste.

decorated with images of the goddess. Eros is also linked to ducks. In the British Museum there is a glazed vase in the shape of a duck with the god of love riding on top of it. Seeing that the duck was sacred to Aphrodite, Eros and even Priapus, it is hardly surprising that the meat of the duck was believed by the Ancient Greeks to be endowed with aphrodisiac properties. For this reason Greek women wore necklaces and brooches in the shape of ducks, which were presumably similar apparel to the lace underwear or daring mini skirts of today.

Oddly enough our sweet feathered friends also symbolized conjugal happiness and fidelity. There is a bronze bed at Pompei with one end in the shape of a duck's head. There is also a duck with much the same significance in a fresco from Pompei preserved in the Museum of Naples. Similarly, the Chinese have the custom of giving a pair of geese to newly weds as a good luck token.

Geese live in a society made up almost entirely of couples. A wild goose without a mate is not a true representative of its species. A pair of geese that prove successful at rearing young may stay together for years. Sometimes their partnership lasts throughout their lives. Lorenz tells a story that helps us to believe in the goose's fidelity. A gander called Florian paired up with a goose called Nat. One day Nat must have been taken from her nest by a fox for on the river bank there were clear signs of Florian's desperate struggle to defend his mate. Similarly, during the incubation period the gander is strictly dedicated to his family role. He keeps guard some distance from the nest and as soon as the eggs start to hatch he comes up closer and presides over the immediate surroundings. Lorenz's story of Ada, the proud and pugnacious widow, is also fascinating. She was married for a second time to a gander

The golden goose, or duck, is an archetypical figure in fairy tales. It features particularly in stories from northern cultures where it is held to symbolize abundance. The china duck opposite is truly golden. Below: a painted porcelain duck from Thailand.

called Fasold. Soon Ada became jealous of Pummelchen, a little goose who used to follow her husband around. Ada's jealousy made her so argumentative that she used to pick quarrels with everyone, even the ganders. She was always fighting with one particular gander called Syrrhaptes but her own partner, Fasold, at least twice defended her from Syrrhaptes' attacks. Lorenz's stories say it all: once married, geese are inseparable. Humankind could well follow their example.

The goose was regarded just as highly by the Ancient Greeks as the swan. In its earliest form the myth of Leda and the Swan relates that Zeus transformed himself into a swan in order to make love to Tyndareus's wife. In a later version Apollodorus adds that Leda herself became a goose for the occasion. After their union Leda produced some eggs. Some versions of the myth relate that the Dioscuri, or "young sons of Zeus," issued from the eggs and others say that there was only one egg and that it contained Castor.

The Ancient Greeks saw the goose as a source of light to illuminate man's arduous journey in search of himself. The "Goose Game" was played very seriously in Athens and

even today games such as Snakes and Ladders are based on
it. The progress of the game represented the path to
enlightenment. The bridge, the prison and the labyrinth
represented obligatory stages in the evolution of the spirit.
Death, on the other hand, signified death of the soul (rather
than physical death, which was seen as a liberation) and
meant going right back to the beginning and starting all
over again. The game is supposed to be for children yet
there are many hidden truths to be found and interpreted by
the more discerning player.

For the Romans the image of the duck belonged to the
magical world of childhood. It is almost certain that the
white, blue and pink glass ducks excavated at Cuma came
from a child's room. Plautus tells us that in patrician families
pet ducks were given to the children as playmates.

Some Native American tribes used to perform a "duck
dance" to ensure a good catch when they went duck
hunting. During their dance nembers of the Kutchin tribe
would flap their arms up and down as if in flight while the
Iroches preferred to shout "quack quack." The dance
movements were similar in both versions of the ritual. The
men stood in a double circle, forming a double line of

arches. The women danced inside the circles, playing the part of the ducks caught by the skilled huntsmen. The duck dance or "waima" was part of the "hesi" cycle performed by Native Americans in present day California. This means that it was part of one of three cults practised by the tribes in this area. This particular cult was centered on the ritual of dance. The men let out high screams as they stood in their circles and gradually they were joined by other dancers impersonating the spirit of abundance. All of them waddled continuously in imitation of our feathered friends.

Still on the Pacific coast, the Kwakiutl narrate the story of the mink, born to a girl who became pregnant when the warm rays of the sun fell upon her belly. What has the mink to do with our friends the ducks? Well, the mink was named "Born-to-be-the-sun." When he grew up he attempted to take over from his father who, incidentally, could not wait to retire. His efforts were so disastrous that he was thrown out of his father's palace in the skies and

The hansa *in wood below comes from northern India and was made during the nineteenth century. The modern duck opposite was also made from wood in India. It looks as though it is floating about on its pond deep in thought.*

No airs and graces among the Anatidae family – the farmyard duck poses as a salt cellar and sits quite at ease with its more refined companions from China and Denmark.

warned never to return. Alone and desperate, Born-to-be-the-sun began to search the rivers of the world for a mate. Given the sort of creature that he was, this venture was bound to be unsuccessful. He met beavers, frogs, water beetles, coots, divers... It always went well at the beginning but then, somehow, he would get fed up. He would fall in love at first sight but, after a brief honeymoon period, he would brutally abandon his mate and go off in search of fresh excitement. In the end he met his match, in the form, needless to say, of a duck. And this is what happened. One day Born-to-be-the-sun and Madame Duck were gliding along together when he saw some minnows below the surface of the water. Seized by feverish greed he dived down and gobbled them up. When he returned to the surface Madame Duck begged him to go down again and eat his fill: "Stay just as long as you like, my darling," she said. The fact is Madame could hardly wait to escape from her idiotic suitor who was, it has to be said, a terrible bore. When Born-to-be-the-sun bobbed up again his beloved was nowhere to be seen. From that moment he gave up any further attempts to find a partner. One cannot help suspecting that all the female creatures of the river had assigned the duck to give the mink his come-uppance – a task that she performed with admirable finesse. It is very satisfying that the simple duck should beat the aristocratic mink at his own game.

There is also a legend from northern Siberia concerning a duck. When God was in the process of creating the world he realized that he was running out of the necessary materials, so he sent the duck and the coot off to find some more mud for him. This is when the duck's inherent sense of responsibility and helpful nature come to the fore and

A rare and precious decoy duck dating from the end of the nineteenth century. It is made from very light wood, designed to float on water like a real wild duck.

indeed show up the ineptitude of the coot. The duck came back with a good quantity of mud in her beak while the coot did not manage to bring back anything at all. God was angry with the coot. With her long beak she should have been able to return with even more mud than the duck. As a consequence of this episode the coot was condemned to live forever on the water and to feed off waste matter on the river bed.

Our feathered friends appear on tombs in Rhodes. They are also carved on Etruscan tombs in Italy and Celtic ones in Germany. One Celtic example is to be found at Hallstatt-Latene near Sigmaringen. To the Celts the symbolic significance of the goose was very similar to that of the swan. Like her noble cousin she was seen as a messenger from the supernatural world. In *De Bello Gallico* Caesar relates that the ancient Britons were forbidden to eat geese. They were purely for pleasure or as the Romans, experts in this field, would have said, *voluptatis causa*.

The Babylonians were rich and able merchants. They measured out their goods using weights made of bronze or stone. This tradition had been passed from the Samarians to the Assyrians. The bronze weights were in the shape of lions and the stone ones were carved in the shape of ducks. The type of stone used varied according to the weight. Small weights were ducklings made from hematite and the heaviest weights were hewn from large lumps of rock, often carved into the shape of a duck resting with its head under its wing. The lion understandably had close symbolic links with some divine being. Given the symbolic stature of the lion, it is probable that the duck who shared

A duck salt cellar in sandalwood from Madagascar. In this pose it could be searching for the mud needed to make the world, as the ancient legend goes.

his responsibilities was also linked to a divine figure.

Aristotle and Pliny both made detailed studies of ducks and reached the conclusion that they were natural weather forecasters. They noticed how these birds behaved in particular ways before a change in the weather. For example, repeated diving meant that it would rain; when they preened their feathers with their beaks and flapped their wings vigorously, it meant that the wind was increasing.

In 1913 a German academic called Otto Keller wrote a book called *The Ancient World of Animals*. This was a rich and fascinating study of the symbolic uses made of different beasts by various cultures through the ages. The duck has had a variety of different names and some of them have influenced the terms used to describe different sorts of boats. For example, Varro called them *amphibia*, because they could travel by land or water. Ausonius called

The duck above is Japanese. It is an ivory button known as a netsuke, made in the nineteenth century. The duck-shaped papier-mâché jewellery box opposite is from India. The ducks on the previous pages come from Bali and are carved from turquoise. At every latitude the duck is seen as a symbolic creature.

them *remipedi*, or "oar feet," because their feet functioned like oars in the water. So far so good, but at this point Keller enters into a feverish search for philological links. He compares the German *Kahn* (boat) with the French *cane* (female duck) and *canard* (drake). There is no stopping him; he even invites us to note the curious similarity between the Rumanian word *raẓe*, (duck) and the Latin *ratis* (raft).

Keller does tell us some interesting, and slightly less tenuous, things about certain species of duck. For example, to the ancient Mongolian tribes and their neighbours the Kalmucks, the ruddy shield duck was sacred on account of its high pitched whistle in flight (its call is similar to the sound made by a clarinet and it carries over huge distances). Additionally, the coloured plumage resembled the clothes worn by the shaman, or priest. The Pontus duck also had a sacred significance. In Classical Antiquity it was said to be poisonous and, as Plinius himself confirms, this gave it an important position in the contemporary pharmacopoeia. The fact that other inhabitants of the "Pontus," which means sea, were also considered poisonous leads one to suspect that this association of sea creatures and poison was in some way linked with Mithridates. Mithridates, king of the Pontus, took poison himself in gradually increasing doses as a form of immunization against its unpleasant effects. And hence the word "mithridatism," or immunity to a poison having become accustomed to it after the intake of gradually increasing doses. The blood of the Pontus duck was thought to have healing properties and was perhaps used as a midway between homeopathic and shock treatment.

The wigeon is a maritime creature. It is sometimes known as the Penelope duck on account of its links with the Penelope of Classical Antiquity. Her parents, who were obviously not very loving, planned to make a sacrifice of her by throwing her into the sea. The tale has been incorporated into numerous fairy stories. The heroine of the stories is always a queen or a princess that has been turned into a duck as the result of a wicked spell. The Afanasyev tales tell the story of a wicked witch–serpent who turns a princess into a white duck. The princess-duck lays three eggs that hatch to produce three little children. The witch–serpent, as sly as ever, casts a spell over them as they sleep, transforming them into three ducklings. Not content with that, she kills them. The princess-duck, now a truly tragic figure, manages to fly to the palace of her royal husband. She sings him a little song: "Quack, quack, quack, my little ones/ Quack, quack, quack, my ducklings/ The old witch has killed them/ The old witch, the wicked serpent/ The sly wicked serpent/ She has drowned them in the rapids/ She has turned them into little white ducklings." The Prince responded with a magic spell: "Get thee behind me old tree, pretty girl spring up for me." At once, the tree grew up behind the prince and, before his very eyes, the white duck was transformed into his own wife, the princess

again. Later on in the tale he forces the witch, mainly by sheer bullying because he was out of magic words, to bring his children back to life.

Another story from the Afanasyev collection serves to confirm our view of ducks as a source of riches and abundance. There were two orphaned brothers who found a duck in its nest among the roots of a birch tree. On alternate days the duck laid a golden egg in the morning and a silver one in the evening. On her breast were written the following words: "He who eats my head will become king, he who eats my heart will have gold pour from his mouth." The boys took the duck home to cook it. When they arrived their stepmother, behaving in the traditional manner

of all fairy-tale stepmothers, would not even consider cooking the duck for them. In the end, however, the boys managed to eat the duck or, to be more precise, one ate its head and the other its heart. They escaped from the wicked stepmother and after a long walk they arrived at a crossroads where there was a notice with the following words: "He who turns right (to the east) will become king. He who turns left (to the west) will become rich." The two brothers went their separate ways and the duck's prophecy was fulfilled. Another good deed accomplished by our friend.

In numerous Slavic tales the golden egg causes the death of the witch or the monster and brings prosperity to the young hero or heroine. It is not only the goose that lays golden eggs or has golden feathers. In Slavic and Oriental fairy-tales and legends ducks and geese frequently exchange roles — almost as though there was no difference between the two species. We know that there are enormous differences, but ornithological detail is of little importance to the folkloric imagination.

There is a German tale about a hunter who shoots an enormous goose. When he goes into the thicket to retrieve it, he finds that a beautiful naked woman has taken its place. The same tale is related in other countries, but a duck stands in for the goose. It would be better if this story did not get around, for our feathered friends have enough to fear at the hands of the hunters as it is. Imagine their fate if huntsmen the world over believed that every dead goose or duck would be transformed into a young and sensuous woman!

Opposite: a table with a theme. The glass salt cellar was made in Italy in the 1940s. The silver place name holder also comes from Italy. The wooden napkin ring is Polish and the butter knives are Japanese. Below: an English duck made in the 1960s.

Not only golden eggs

In 1914 a beautiful story about the adventures of a wild goose was printed in a French magazine called *La Semaine de Suzette*. After many vicissitudes a goose arrived, tired and hungry, in a farmyard. Here she was welcomed with open wings by her domesticated cousins who extolled the comforts of their farmyard existence. The wild goose soon became accustomed to her new way of life and began to enjoy living on the farm. This went on until she realized that they were only allowed all the food they wanted because they were all being fattened for the pot. At this point she flew away, calling to her friends as she went: "You stay here and gorge yourselves, my friends. I prefer my own sparse meals in the freedom of the marshes."

Yet for geese and ducks liberty has always been an ephemeral thing. Whether they are raised in captivity or live in the wild, they must fear for their lives. Fattened for the meat market or brought down by a hunter, they are always exploited to the last little feather and ounce of flesh. Since ancient times the meat of the duck and goose has been held

in high regard. According to the *Odyssey* even Penelope kept geese in her old age. She had about twenty of them and she fattened them up on corn mash. Goose eggs were popular too. A coin found at Eion in Macedonia shows a goose laying an egg. Maybe it was a golden one like the goose's egg in Aesop's Fables.

It was the Romans, however, who really cultivated the fashion for eating ducks and geese. White German geese were the most popular candidates for the pot, followed by

the Gallic variety. They were incredibly resilient creatures and rather than being transported to Rome in cages, they were driven on foot over the Alps by goose-boys. This was quite an achievement for an animal that has always been laughed at for its wobbly and somewhat unsure gait. According to Martial only the front end of the duck was to be eaten while the hind end should be left for the servants. Goose liver was seen as a delicacy and the Romans learned to enlarge it by feeding the goose with a mixture of flour, milk and honey. As for wildfowl feathers, these were used for stuffing cushions and mattresses and the poor creatures were plucked twice a year for this purpose. Naturally, as well as the Romans, the inhabitants of colder parts in Northern Europe used feathers to stuff quilts, while some Native American tribes used them as ceremonial ornaments. Today the best feathers for quilts and padded jackets come from the eider duck. Goose feathers were used for writing much later. In fact, the first mention of quills goes back to the fifth century A.D.

At moulting time ducks and geese abandon flight and go about on foot. The Samoyeds and the other inhabitants of Siberia took advantage of this period to fill their larders with enough meat to feed themselves and their dogs for an entire year. After they were killed, the birds, some of which had been plucked, were put into a pit. The frozen earth all around them worked as a primitive freezer. When the hot weather came, the meat was cut into strips, salted and left to dry in the sun.

At the time of the Roman Empire there were elaborate recipes for cooking duck. They used vinegar, oil and honey to create a sweet and sour effect that was probably delicious. Marcus Terrentius Varro was employed by Caesar to look

Talking of ducks, one cannot help thinking of their gastronomic role. Here is a duck at table again, fortunately in the form of a silver-plated cheese knife.

71

Above: a multi-coloured wooden sculpture from Bali. Opposite: a splendid old Italian decoy duck. If you shake this duck, you can hear the lead pellets that have ended up inside rattling around.

after the public library in Rome. In his notebooks he gave a precise description of the habits and customs of his fellow Romans. He also gave a detailed account of the artificial ponds used for raising ducks at his own home: "... The pond must have a supply of fresh water running through it. This serves both to keep it clean and to bring food to the ducks." He then gives a meticulous list of all the things that ducks should and should not eat, and continues: "The pond must be fenced in so that the ducks cannot escape and predators cannot break in. . . At the center of the pond there should be aquatic plants to provide shade and shelter. The lining of the pond should be made from cement so that it will be free from weeds or algae." All in all, should we decide to raise ducks in our own back yard, we only have to read the writings of this erudite Roman to make sure we are doing everything correctly.

What about the medicinal qualities of ducks and geese? Some doctors, such as Galen, warned against the indigestible qualities of duck and goose. Cato the Censor, on the other hand, considered the meat so beneficial that he used to give it to his children when they were unwell. Goose fat was widely used to treat skin diseases and colic. It was also the basis of many ointments.

Despite Varro's instructions on domestic duck rearing, we know that ever since the days of the ancient Romans it has been more common to hunt ducks than to rear them. This is partly because the meat of the wild duck has more flavour than that of its domestic counterpart and of goose.

Decoy ducks were already in use in Roman times. Today they are either made beautifully out of wood and then painted or, less attractively from plastic. Used in combination with a decoy duck call, they lure the ducks into the range of the hunters concealed in their hides.

Autumn is the optimum season for shooting wild ducks and geese. This is when they are migrating from north to south. They are often shot while having a rest on a pond en route. It is not surprising that in some areas the duck has become a symbol of autumn. Several clothes manufacturers use a duck as their trademark as the duck is a symbol of the warm colours and soft materials used to make shoes, jackets

and jerseys for the onset of the cold season. It is at this time of year that an abundance of ducks and geese should be brought to our tables, or so a saying of the Piedmontese of northern Italy goes: "Put geese, chestnuts and wine away, and keep them until Saint Martin's day." The saint's day falls in mid autumn, on November 11. The goose has special links with Saint Martin, a sainted bishop who is particularly important in France. Legend has it that it was geese that revealed to everybody with their calls the place where the saint hid himself when he did not want to become a bishop. November 11 is also New Year's Day for the Celts. The Celts held the goose to be a sacred creature. They even took it with them when they visited their pagan shrines. When Saint Martin went to the Celts as a missionary, he wasted no time in vetoing the bird's sacred status.

Is it purely coincidental, furthermore, that the name Martin means "dedicated to Mars," just like his friends and enemies the geese? Perhaps it is. It is no coincidence, however, that German children celebrate the Festival of the Lanterns on November 11 as well. The festival marks the beginning of deep winter and all the darkness and restrictions that it brings. The children celebrate with songs, fires, lanterns and, of course, a goose, to exorcize the winter season. The goose may be a real one or a toy. It symbolizes abundance and good luck for the duration of the dark months.

Saint Martin must have been a powerful figure. The Merovingians who ruled France between the fifth and eighth centuries even named a specific era after him. It began on the day of his death. It can have been no coincidence that the Merovingians had a goose as the mascot for their troops. To understand this we must first

look at the secret behind their swords which were famous throughout medieval Europe. It has been discovered that contemporary artisans were capable of purifying iron hundreds of years before our own modern methods were invented. This enabled them to forge swords from pure steel. To turn iron into steel it must be carburized. In order to do this they invented a cementation process using carbon-rich organic matter. But what was it? The Arab chronicles of the ninth century contain an ancient German legend in which it is said that the Franks gave their geese a mixture of flour and iron filings to eat. Their excrement was then used to forge the famous steel swords. A careful chemical analysis of the blades confirms the truth of the legend. They have been found to contain both carbon and azote. Modern experts confirm that, given the high carbon and azote content of goose excrement, the geese themselves were certainly important agents in the process of cementation. The art of forging steel had been invented

The modern ceramic duck above is Oriental.
The one opposite comes from the Irish island
of Aran. In light stone, it is depicted in what
Konrad Lorenz described as its "submissive
pose."

and, under careful tuition, the goose soon became master of
it.

Let it be said once and for all: they can do more than
just lay golden eggs. These accounts of our friends'
achievements perhaps lack the romance of Aesop's tale, but
in compensation they are all real-life stories, revealing the
useful gifts given to ungrateful humans. They serve as a
testimony to the fact that ducks and geese are always on our
side and always ready to give us all that they have. Some
Native American tribes of Canada even used their beaks as
moulds for maple-syrup cookies.

Recipes for cooking duck are always rich and luxurious.
A good cook can distinguish between an autumn duck and a
spring one. The autumn duck is larger and fattier and should
be accompanied by rich ingredients with a strong flavour. It

is excellent, and very popular, cooked with orange. Spring ducks are young, small and tender and they have a more delicate flavour that suits roasting. They are best served with spring vegetables. Chinese Peking duck with its sweet and sour sauce is also a delicacy.

Humans, as we know, are never satisfied. It is reputed that hundreds of years ago they even invented vegetarian ducks that grew on trees. This strange story appears in a book called *Topographia Hibernia*, written in 1187 by Giraldus Cambrensis. He writes about certain birds called *bernacae* that were to be found in large quantities in Ireland. Here is his description: "Nature produces them, contrary to her own laws, in a most extraordinary manner. They are like marsh ducks but a little bit smaller. They grow in the guise of growths on the trunks of fir trees that have been

washed up on to the beach by the sea. As they develop, they

hold on to the trunk with their beaks like seaweed adheres
to wood on the beach. Shells protect them so that they can
grow freely underneath. In the course of time they become
covered by a layer of feathers and eventually the birds drop
off into the water or fly into the air. They feed on the sap
from the tree or from the sea itself. I have seen more than a
thousand of these little birds with my own eyes. They were
hanging from a tree trunk on the beach, lying under their
shells and already formed." The author then observes that
"Certain bishops and prelates in Ireland eat these creatures
during Lent because they are not made from meat." This
raises the suspicion that the whole idea of vegetable ducks
may have been invented by Catholic priests who had no
intention of renouncing their rich diets during Lent but
this would be too simple an explanation. In any case, Pope
Innocent III evidently banned the consumption of *bernacae*
during Lent in 1215. One would expect this to put a
definitive end to discussions about vegetable ducks but this
was not the case. The legend continued for several
centuries, fed by academics and travellers alike. Perhaps one
of the motives behind these discussions was the constant
research into the miracles of creation in order to
understand the manifestation of the divine in every aspect
of life. They even went as far as citing Aristotle himself,
claiming that this great philosopher had seen or at least
written about "birds that grow on trees and are called
bernacae." Needless to say, Aristotle never even dreamt of
writing on the subject.

In the middle of the fifteenth century one of the earliest
books to be printed was the *Buch der Natur* or "Book of
Nature," written by Von Megenberg (or Von Megensburg,
the spelling is uncertain). The book contained a description

of vegetable ducks that "grew on a tree with several branches from which these creatures sprouted. They are smaller than geese. Their feet are the same as a duck's but they are black. They hang on to the bark or trunk of the tree with their beaks. At a certain point they fall into the sea where they continue to develop until they can fly."

So, do these vegetable ducks grow on dead tree trunks washed up on the shore or, like fruit, on the branches of living trees? In 1597 the mystery began to unfold with a glimmer of truth that emerged from *Gerard's Herbal* printed in London during that year. This was more than a century after Von Megenberg's book had been published, but things were different in those days. News travelled slowly and television had not been invented to reduce world events to the daily items that we now devour and then forget. To return to Gerard, he reported that "In the north of Scotland there are trees that produce a sort of reddish white sea snail. Inside their shells there are tiny, living ducks that we call *bernacae*. . . Those that fall to the ground are destroyed. . . the trees then sprout and at the beginning of the summer the ducks, complete with feathers, are to be seen."

Then finally in the eighteenth century the enigma was solved when the existence of two separate animals was established. They were very different, although they did share some vaguely similar characteristics which is what had caused all the confusion. The duck was one of them and was of the common Irish variety. The shell, which some claimed was the vegetable duck in its larval stage, was simply a barnacle. It was a barnacle, a crustacean that adheres to rocks or tree trunks close to the water using a tough peduncle, that was mistaken for the duck's beak! A tuft of thread-like appendages blossoms from the shell and this had looked like plumage.

Apart from these tenuous similarities, why did the legend always refer to the wild duck? In 1864 the linguist Max Müller came up with a possible explanation. The birds in question originated in Ireland known as *Hibernia* in Latin. Irish ducks would therefore be known as *Hiberniculae*. The *Lepas anatifera*, or crustacean, was called *Bernacula* in Latin, thus creating the ideal conditions for linguistic ambiguity. With one syllable too few or one too many the *bernaculae* became the larval stage of the duck, and from this mistake a legend was born.

This duck–goose in painted terracotta was made in Apulia, southern Italy. Opposite: the tree of vegetable ducks taken from the Histoire admirable des herbes émerveillables *by Duret in 1605.*

A clever idea from the Ramada chain of hotels in England. This plastic duck with its comic expression is to be found in every one of their bathrooms. A session with this aquatic friend leaves even the tiredest business person laughing and relaxed. For a small price you can take it home with you or, better still, have it mailed in its own box with air holes and straw.

My darling, my duck

Here is an interesting piece of information, which may be of interest to our female readers. If a young man from Siberia or central Asia goes all misty eyed on you and starts to call you his "goose," be warned, he is referring to the girl of his dreams. In place of the usual references along the lines of: "She may be pretty, but she's a silly little goose," he will be talking about her with sighs and soulful eyes.

In ancient China a prospective lover would send a live duck or goose to the woman he desired. The message implied by this gift was simple. She was required to abandon her prudish attitudes and embark on the activities undertaken by the feathered messenger each spring.

In Greek and Roman plays we find the wildfowl words *neissarion* and *aneticula* used as terms of endearment. Of course, "ducks" and "ducky" are used in the same way in England today.

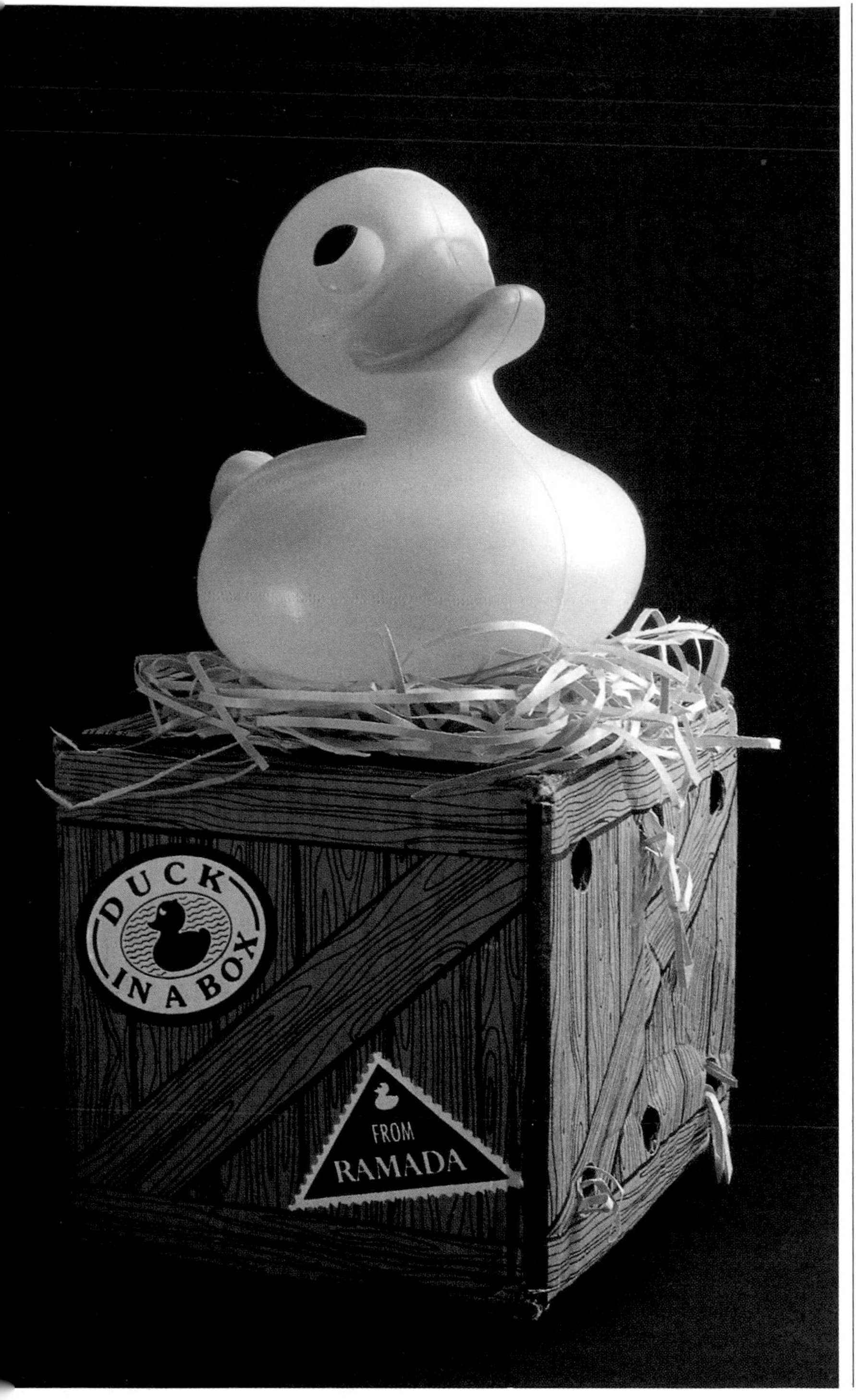
DUCK IN A BOX
FROM
RAMADA

While we are on the subject of endearing ducks, see if you can guess who this dear, muddle-headed duck is. He is a little bit hysterical, a bit neurotic, rather timid and very lazy, but nonetheless he is loved by children between the ages of nine and ninety all over the world. He is constantly involved in the most ridiculous adventures from which he emerges looking bruised and foolish. He is usually covered with plasters, which appear as if by magic during the course of his fights and accidents. (Where does he keep them? Who puts them on for him?) I am sure you have already guessed who he is, but if not: he wears a sailor suit and he has a large family that are both a bane to him and a salvation. Yes! You've got it, it is the great, the eternal Donald Duck.

He first appeared in a short called *The Wise Little Hen* in 1934. Since then he has made innumerable films. In the old days he was slightly thinner, his neck was longer and his beak was sharper. He was created in a rather unusual way; his voice came first and then his body. It sounds very strange but this is how it all began. Walt Disney heard Clarence

Above: a tiny, delicately painted tea pot in
Chinese porcelain. "Tea for one" but with
our little friend for company. Opposite: a
fork holder in the shape of a duck. It is
carved out of olive wood and looks rather
prim.

Nash doing his "duck voice." It was so effective that Disney
decided to create a cartoon duck to go with it. Judging by
Donald Duck's success, Disney had, as usual, made exactly
the right decision. Later on Donald Duck took on the
appearance that we know so well today. He became
rounder (which was quite correct if you consider his
origins, and, of course, his famous joke, "Me, in an egg?"),
his beak became shorter and rounder and his huge eyes
began at the base of his beak.

The Ugly Duckling is a wonderful story, written perhaps
for adults more than children. Certain aspects of it
are rather perplexing. Educational psychologists are not

This sweet little duck was produced in Germany in the 1950s. The couple on the preceding pages is endearing too. The warm, terracotta colours are those of their country of origin, Mexico.

convinced that the tale has educative value as it may give the child a false vision of reality. In the tale it is as though, while our fate is already written, we can allow ourselves the luxury of daydreaming and can expect our dearest wishes to come true with little effort on our part.

However, we could look at the ugly duckling in a different light. As duck lovers it may seem a rather hypocritical light but the problem lies in the duckling's behaviour. Our friend is very proud and chooses not to make any compromises. He is different from everyone else and everyone else rejects him but, who knows, perhaps he rejected and shunned them too. The little duckling escapes from one situation after another. First it is the yard, then the marshes and then the barn – a journey that no doubt represents a search for himself. This process undoubtedly turns him into a hero and a character for whom we feel immediate sympathy and affection. But it must be said that this funny little character, who some people believe represents Hans Christian Andersen himself, does very little to bring about his own transformation into a swan. To tell the truth, he does nothing at all. Andersen was a poor shoemaker's son who struggled long and hard to achieve his new position in society. He became "a swan" because he worked hard while the ugly duckling did not even have to try. It might be more realistic to say that the author of the tale was an ugly duckling who grew up into a fine duck through a process of personal development.

Today our newspapers are full of ugly ducklings who have grown up into beautiful ducks. When Andersen was alive things were very different. Trying to free oneself from

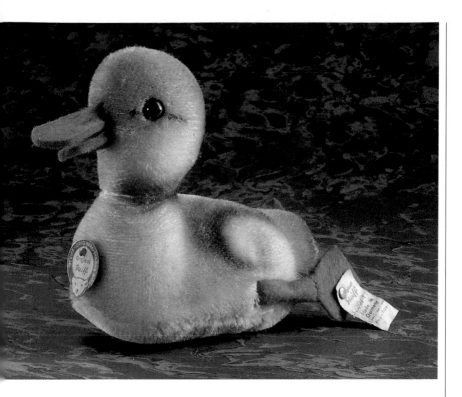

the position of social underdog was a desperate task. The Danish writer would not have believed it possible to achieve a new social status by virtue of one's own efforts alone. The change would have to be predestined. One would have to be, unwittingly, a swan through and through from the very beginning. So for Andersen's autobiographical metaphor he required a hero, for which he chose the biggest and most radiant of the legendary *hansa*.

For us, the swan is a divine and mythical bird but actually its value is purely aesthetic. You cannot even eat it – it is just a beautiful ornament. What is more, swans can be very aggressive. Nevertheless, the story of the ugly duckling is very moving. It is the tale of a person who undergoes a thousand and one misfortunes. At last he finds that he has been transformed into a fantastic creature. He is suddenly a member of the family that he had always dreamt of belonging to and, as we all know, anything is possible in a fairy tale. Reality is quite different. In truth we have more affinity with ducks than swans and, fortunately, we no longer live in the dark ages when survival depended on acts of enormous courage. We live in a society where, for most people, the problem of survival has been replaced by different and subtler discomforts and worries. Today we are plagued by anxiety, stress and the speed of life. We long for moments of peace, relaxation and happiness. Ducks bring happiness and make us smile. For the past two years a chain of hotels in England has put a duck in every one of its bathrooms to keep the guests company. If one of these plastic ducks makes a business person smile at the end of a long day's work, it has done its job. If the guests' enthusiasm is anything to go by, the experiment seems to be working very well. Many people actually ask if they can take the duck away with them. For a modest price the hotel is willing to pack the duck up and send it to the client's home address, even if it is abroad. There is no difficulty as far as the duck is concerned – there are air holes in the packaging and a layer of straw is provided for him to sit on!

If we look back over all the ducks mentioned in this

Another tin toy from Taiwan: a wind-up duck that does better on land than in water. Opposite: a duck compass made by an Italian company that chose the duck as the symbol of their range of colourful and water-proof products.

book, starting with the plastic ones in English hotel bathrooms, then Donald and Daffy and all the other cartoon ducks, the clothes labels, duck teapots, paper clips, candle sticks, jewellery and ornaments, all in the shape of ducks, finally we arrive back at the real thing, fluttering about on our ponds and in our parks. There can be no doubt that the duck is more representative of our age than the swan.

We are ducklings awaiting a miraculous transformation into beautiful ducks. As inhabitants of the industrialized world we can achieve this transformation but it will not happen if we just wait, passively, for a miraculous metamorphosis to leave us in the shape of a swan.

The swan is beautiful, regal and magnificent but it is also distant and uncommunicative. Faced by an adult swan we feel a bit nervous and unsure. This is hardly surprising, for the very idea of stroking or cuddling them is out of the question. The swan's regal character leaves us feeling slightly inferior and its beauty takes our breath away. That is just it, could you have a really close relationship with a swan? Could you achieve the same relationship with a swan that some naturalists have experienced with wild geese? Who knows, if it were perhaps a little less haughty... Our response to ducks, on the other hand, is immediate. We spontaneously want to stroke those fluffy little golden yellow goslings and to play with those colourful, garrulous adults ducks. Of all the *hansa* the duck is the happiest, the

most carefree and, above all, the most approachable. We do not live in heroic times, but there is more justice in the world. For better for for worse, these are fine times for ducks.

Over the years Donald Duck has been drawn by numerous animators. Carl Barks was the first. He wrote and drew more than five hundred stories. He had a particularly clear image of the duck's psychology. His Donald was a sort of hero–anti-hero with disasters raining down on him in a constant stream. Donald went on searching, despite everything, for the lucky break that would change his life. Sometimes things went well for a while, but his luck never lasted. Fortunately he was too lazy to grieve over his disasters – his outlook demanded maximum results for minimum outlay. We could recognize his frustrations and neuroses as our own or, should we refuse to admit it, we could at least compare them to those of our next door neighbour. Perhaps this is why Umberto Eco, the Italian academic and novelist, said that he would only talk about Donald Duck in the presence of his analyst! In fact the whole, large family of Disney ducks and geese serve as an interesting reflection of human foibles.

Donald himself is the archetypal rich miser who will not sacrifice one penny of his worldly goods. It is no coincidence that Bark, his creator, referred to him as Scrooge. And who is Gladstone if not the friend who we envy because everything always goes right for him? Grandma Duck is obviously the perfect grandmother that we all dreamt of having. Incidentally, have you noticed that even Disney muddles up ducks and geese? Donald Duck has a relation called Gander. Gladstone is also a member of the Gander family and little Gus has Goose as his surname. If we look back through the ages departing from Donald and his family to the *hansa* or duck-goose of ancient Sanskrit, it seems that the confusion between the two aquatic creatures has always existed. There is obviously far more to it than first suspected.

Daffy Duck is another great personality from the world of cartoons. He has black feathers and is most definitely a wild duck. He is just as vain and arrogant as his white friend Donald, but he is much more independent. The most important thing about him is that he always has a goal that he pursues with all his strength.

Daffy was born in 1937 when he starred in Tex Avery's cartoon: *Porky's Duck Hunt*. Like Donald he has altered over the years, becoming thinner and more angular. Along with his shape, his character has changed and he is, if possible, even more aggressive than before.

Real ducklings are endearing creatures. Their large heads appear too big for their bodies. Their cheeks are plump, their eyes are large and their bodies are soft and cuddly. These features combine to arouse our most tender and protective instincts. It is the same feeling that we experience when we encounter tiny babies or puppies. Konrad Lorenz, who knew a good deal about ducks and geese, as well as human behaviour, demonstrated how the young of each could evoke the same reactions in us.

Daffy Duck, with his black feathers, is a different creature altogether. Rather than arousing tender feelings in the audience, he inspires confidence, showing us how good he is at coping in any situation, however awkward. He may be a little mad, but he has always been anything but "daffy" or

Above: a novel Chinese duck in painted wood. Opposite: a mother duck and her duckling carved out of wood. With their simple outline, they swim imperturbably on their imaginary pond.

daft. In *Duck Soup to Nuts* for example, made in 1944, Daffy torments poor Porky the hunter so much so that Daffy becomes the aggressor and Porky becomes the artless victim.

That shameless duck even has the nerve to shout at Porky over the muzzle of his gun. "Put that gun down," he yells. "You aren't looking at any old duck to be served up at table. I'm too clever for you. I'm a genius. I can sing!" (He sings a couple of verses from a recent number.) "I can dance!" (He dances a series of exuberant pirouettes.) "And I'm an actor as well! I've got a contract with Warner Brothers." Daffy then becomes completely submerged in the role of the "bad guy" and attacks poor Porky who has no alternative but to run away from the enraged duck.

Yes, Daffy is impulsive. Unlike Donald Duck he has no

Model ducks are commonly used for decorative purposes. This one was made in France during the 1930s. It was made from plaster and then expertly polished.

inhibitions and he is practical and enterprising. His main fault is that he is without any form of self-control, but Warner transforms this fault into a virtue. Daffy was still allowed to do what he liked, but when he lost his temper he did it with the enemy. During the Second World War there were two patriotic cartoons. In *Scrap Happy Daffy* the argumentative duck wages battle against a German goose with expansionist views. In *Plane Daffy* he manages not to fall for the charms of a Nazi duck spy called Hata Mari. By seducing her himself he leaves her powerless. Well done, Daffy!

In 1942, Donald Duck won an Oscar for his performance in a short entitled *Der Führer's Face*. This was a satire about

Brightly painted bamboo leaves have been used to create this splendid example of Chinese workmanship.

the Nazis in which our feathered friend dreamt that he was working in a German munitions factory.

All in all, if Donald is a personification of what we are like, Daffy personifies the person that we would like to be. He has built his defenses well and he will do anything to save his own skin – or should I say feathers – and to secure a place for himself in a hostile world. Yes, he is a James Dean looking for love, a Marlon Brando seeking approval, an insecure person hellbent on proving to himself and everyone else that he is capable of anything.

We humans refuse to recognize that we are like Donald although we most certainly are. We would like to resemble Daffy but, while we would never admit it, we are not able.

A delicate sauce boat made in the form of a duck–swan. The spoon represents the head and neck and the body forms the bowl of the sauce boat. They combine to create one beautifully elegant and original creature.

While on the subject of wanting to be what we are not and refusing to accept what we are, what about *The Ugly Duckling*? This must be one of the most popular fairy tales? One day mother duck looks at the eggs in her nest and realizes that one of them is much bigger than the others. She shows it to a friend who tells her that it has to be a turkey's egg and that the chick will not be able to swim. When the eggs finally hatch the chick is an ugly little thing, quite unlike the beautiful goslings that surround it. However, it turns out to be both sweet-natured and a fine swimmer. When the mother duck introduces her brood to the other ducks on the pond they all turn against the ugly

duckling. They bully him and peck him, saying that he is

"too ugly and too big and deserves to be pecked." Sadly, it is not only in fairy tales that the "odd ones out" are picked on and excluded from the group. Disaster follows disaster until one day in early spring the ugly duckling sees a flock of swans. "They were big, beautiful creatures flying off to warmer climes . . . The ugly duckling felt a curious longing . . . He loved them as he had never loved anything before." After more sadness and torment, finally the next spring the ugly duckling turns into a magnificent swan.

The couple and the family have a fundamental role among the hansa *or wildfowl. This wooden mother, father and duckling trio comes from France.*

Quack, quack in the library

A little bit frivolous, intelligent, usually sweet-natured but sometimes aggressive, sleepy but impulsive, mediocre walkers, fabulous flyers and champion swimmers and divers, symbols of fidelity and adundance, unusual guard dogs and, finally, an emblem of our era. We have said all sorts of things about ducks and geese, but it does not end here – they appear in many other books as well.

Our friends, amongst other things, bring good tidings. This is their role in fairy tales where duck–geese lay golden eggs, have golden feathers or bring riches to anyone who eats them.

Their love of freedom features in many legends and poems. They challenge the skies and the waters, just like the poet who longs to sail high above the earth. Other times, leaving this wild and passionate image behind, they are to be found in various roles in the pages of books. Fluttering with them from one book shelf to another we may be in for some new surprises.

An abundance of ducks in this brightly coloured English wooden letter rack. Despite their modest expressions, these ducks have won a place in the hearts of poets and men of letters.

A letter from Rosa Luxemburg when in prison to Gertrud Zlottko

Rosa Luxemburg, the German Socialist agitator, was assassinated by troops in 1919. These few, desperate lines speak for themselves.

It's a strange thing, but there must be a goose living around here somewhere, a real goose with feathers and everything. Every so often it makes a noise and its cry fascinates me. It's a pity that it happens so rarely. Do you know why I like it so much? The cry of the goose is completely wild, there is nothing domesticated about it. The sound itself speaks of the bird that flies south, it is full of their determination to reach enormous heights and their love of distant parts. When I hear that cry I am filled with a sense of longing. I don't know exactly what it is that I long for. Perhaps I just want to distance myself from the world.

Heavens! If only I could fly off like a wild goose!

AESOP, **The Goose with the Golden Eggs**

Thinking to get at once all the gold that the goose could give, he killed it, and opened it only to find – nothing.

Two famous ducks: on this page, Daffy Duck, a terrible rascal from Warner Brother Productions; opposite, Inspector Canardo by the Belgian designer Benot Sokal. He is the hero of a series of tough detective stories.

GOOSEY, GOOSEY, GANDER, **Traditional Nursery Rhyme**

Goosey, goosey, gander
   Whither shall I wander?
Upstairs and downstairs
And in my lady's chamber.

HANS CHRISTIAN ANDERSEN, **Fairy tales**

There are two episodes in The Ugly Duckling *that we must look at. One is the point at which the ugly duckling finally sees the light of day; the other is his official presentation in the yard.*

At last the great big egg cracked open.
"Pip, pip," said the little bird and he
clambered out. He was very big and ugly.
The duck looked at him:
   "This duckling is a frightening size," she
said.
   "He doesn't look like any of the others.
He must be a turkey chick! Hmmm! I
know just what we'll do. Let's throw him
into the water and see what he does!"

The ugly duckling gets on very well indeed in the water. He becomes part of the family and when his brothers and sisters are presented at the farmyard he goes too, but not before his mother has taught them all some manners.

"... Move those legs! Go a bit faster if you can. Bow your heads to the old duck down there. He's the most important of them all, he's got Spanish blood, that's why he's so dignified. Can you see the red rag tied around his leg? It's most unusual – the highest honour that can be accorded to a goose. It means that he must be respected by both men and animals. Hurry up! Don't hang back! Well behaved ducklings walk properly, like Mummy and Daddy! Like this, see? Now bow your heads and say: 'quack!' "

All the ducklings did as they were told. The other ducks looked over at them and said loudly:
"Look, look, here comes the whole procession. As if there weren't enough of us already! How frightful! One of the ducklings is dreadfully ugly. We don't want that one living here!" and with this one of them flew at the Ugly Duckling and pecked him on the neck.

HENRIK IBSEN, **The Wild Duck**

In this play by the great Norwegian playwright a wild duck serves as a symbol of the events in the lives of the Ekdal family. It was given to Hedvig, the youngest child, when it was wounded by a hunter. Now it lives in the loft with their other animals. One of the most exciting scenes in the play occurs in the third act when the audience begins to realize that the duck is Hedvig herself, with her dark and troubled past.

GREGERS. ... The wild duck's the most important thing in there, isn't it?
HEDVIG. Oh, yes. She's a real wild bird, you see. That's why I feel sorry for her.

She's got no one to care for, poor thing.
GREGERS. No family like the rabbits.
HEDVIG. No. The hens have got friends they used to be chicks with; but she's been

The biggest family of cartoon ducks. Donald Duck, Grandpa and Grandma duck, Huey, Dewey and Louie and all the other ducks that have been warming the hearts of old and young alike for nearly seventy years.

separated from all her family. And there's so much that's strange about the wild duck. No one knows her. And no one knows where she came from.

GREGERS. And she's been down to the bottom of the deep.

The metaphor of the duck becomes clear when Hedvig realizes that her father is not her real father. She follows the advice of Gregers, the wicked tenant, who tells her to sacrifice her beloved duck in order to prove how much she loves her father.

HEDVIG. The poor wild duck. He can't bear to look at her any longer either. Do you know, he wants to wring her neck!

GREGERS. Oh, I'm sure he won't do that.

HEDVIG. No, but he said it. And I think it was such a horrid thing for father to say. I say a prayer for the wild duck every evening. I pray that she may be delivered from death and from all evil.

GREGERS. And your father wanted to wring the neck of the wild duck, which you love so much?

HEDVIG. No, he said he ought to, but he'd spare her for my sake. That was kind of him, wasn't it?

GREGERS. (*a little closer*) Yes, but what if you now gave up the wild duck for his sake?

HEDVIG. (*rises*) The wild duck?

GREGERS. Yes. Suppose you sacrificed for him the most precious of your possessions – the thing you love most dearly?

HEDVIG. Do you think that would help?

GREGERS. Try it, Hedvig.

HEDVIG. (*quietly, her eyes aglow*). Yes. I will try it.

By the last act the tragedy is complete. It is intolerably degrading for the noble bird, deprived of its liberty, to live in the loft with pigeons and geese. Similarly, sweet, sensible Hedvig cannot tolerate her life in a cold, hypocritical atmosphere. Instead of pointing it at the duck, she turns the gun against herself and shoots herself, dead.

JOHAN WELHAVEN, **The Marine Duck**

Johan Welhaven was Ibsen's favourite poet. He was inspired by these very verses to write The Wild Duck.

A wild duck swims
Along the coast, peacefully.
The clear water plays
about her pure breast.

A hunter arrives, bent
among the slippery rocks
and he shoots, just for fun,
at the beautiful creature.

The duck cannot return
to the warm refuge of her nest

the duck does not want to shout
about her suffering, her pain.

She dives without a sound
to the bottom of the dark fiord,
the cold waves close over her
and she leaves no trace.

In the deep abyss of the sea
the algae grow large and fresh,
she goes to sleep down there,
where the mute fish lives.

GUY DE MAUPASSANT, **The Wild Geese**, in **Verses**

The French writer Guy de Maupassant wrote about reality, dwelling upon all its most banal and tragic details. In his view, the survival instinct was the only thing that really counted. This poem is a good example of his way of seeing things. The "winged triangle" – or wild geese flying to warmer climes – appears in a winter landscape. A gaggle of domestic geese try to imitate them but, sadly, their wings have already become "impotent."

... There is a clamouring on
the horizon;

It gets closer, it arrives, it is a tribe
of geese.

Opposite: Gédéon by the French illustrator Benjamin Rabier. Gédéon was born in 1923. This is a goose in charge of a farmyard of animals, all organized in a strict hierarchy. Below: the wild goose from an illustrated story printed in La Semaine de Suzette *in 1914. The moral of this tale is that hunger and freedom are better than feasting constantly and ending up on the farmer's table.*

They are like an arrow shot from a bow, all
of them with their necks stretched out.
Flying, bewildered and ever
faster.
They pass, lashing the wind with whistling
wings.
The guide who directs these pilgrims
of the air
Beyond the seas, the woods and
the deserts,
As if to urge on their slow
flight,
Every so often gives a shrill
shout.
Like a double ribbon the caravan
sways,
Rumbling strangely, and unfurls across
the sky.
It is a great winged triangle that grows

ever larger
But their imprisoned brothers scattered
over
the fields,
Stiff with cold, walk
with difficulty.
A ragged, whistling girl
drives them,
Those heavy vessels softly
cradled
They hate the cries of the passing
tribe,
They raise their heads and watch
them escaping
The free travellers crossing
the open spaces,
The prisoners suddenly rise up together to
leave
They flap their impotent wings in vain . . .

This delightful watercolour by Beatrix Potter shows Jemima Puddleduck. To look at she is more of a goose than a duck. Whatever she is, she does no honour to her species. The very first time she leaves the farmyard she allows herself to be taken in by a fox and her escape is only due to the help of the farm dogs.

RUDOLF E. RAPSE AND GOTTFRIED A. BÜRGER, **The Adventures of Baron Munchhausen**

As amazing and amusing as ever, the impulsive Baron recounts one of his famous hunting stories in which he is carried home through the air by his own victims.

Today I will tell you another of my hunting stories. It should help you to believe the one that I told you the other day. You will remember that I had enormous success shooting wild ducks after hitting my head very hard on the door post.

On one of my long expeditions in search of game, (in Russia, if I remember rightly, or Finland, or somewhere like that), on a long expedition, (I repeat), I found myself on the edge of a fine lake. I spied a few dozen wild ducks swimming across the water. Unluckily I had only one shot left in my gun and so could not hope to slay more than a single bird. I would fain have had them all, for I could have entertained a good few friends with these, and with great festivity.

Then I recollected that I had a small piece of bacon in my game-bag, a remnant from my own supplies. I attached this to a long dog-lead which I had by me,

which I unravelled and thus lengthened by at least four times. Thereupon I hid myself in the bulrushes by the shore, flung the morsel of meat towards the pond and watched with great pleasure as the nearest duck raced over and devoured it. The others followed on the first one's heels, and since the greasy scrap on the end of the string emerged almost unchewed from the first duck, it was gobbled up by the next one and so on by each duck in turn. In short, the morsel travelled whole through each and every one of the ducks without becoming detached from its thread. Soon they were all strung together like pearls on a necklace. With great satisfaction I drew them into the shore, slung the necklace over my shoulder and set off home.

Since my house was still a good way off, and the burden of such a bevy of ducks became increasingly wearisome, I nearly came to regret having caught so many. But then such an extraordinary thing happened

I was thrown into a great quandary. The ducks, being indeed still very much alive, began as soon as they had recovered from their initial shock, to beat furiously with their wings and took off into the air with myself dangling below. Now some would have found this an exceedingly tricky situation. But I turned the circumstance as best I could to my advantage, by using my coat-tails to steer myself through the air in the direction of my house. When I arrived above it I was able to let myself down without injury. By maneuvering the head of first one duck and then another I descended slowly and gently, and to the great astonishment of my cook, through the chimney of my house and on to the hearth where, fortunately, there was no fire burning.

Household words the world over
A brief glossary of ducks and geese in four languages

English

duck *n.* (from Old English *duce, doke*) small aquatic bird of Anatidae family || (*fig.*) affectionate expression equivalent to dear or sweetheart || (*cricket*) originally *duck's egg*, the zero (0) that records in a scoring sheet that a player made no runs || (*informal.*) *like water off a duck's back*, making no impression || *take to something like a duck to water*, learn to do something or become attracted to something very quickly || (*informal*) *lovely weather for ducks*, rainy or rough weather || (*informal*) *in two shakes of a duck's tail*, in a flash.

DUKW *n.* pronounced *duck* (*military acronym*) an amphibious vehicle used during the Second World War.

ducking stool *n.* (*history*) seat to which suspects, particularly witches, were tied and then immersed in water.

goose *n.* (from Old English *gos*, derived from German *Gans*, sanskrit *hansa*) web-footed, long-necked bird of Anatidae family || (*informal*) a silly individual || *all his geese are swans*, said of somebody who is given to exaggerating the importance of people or things || (*informal*) *to cook one's goose*, to sacrifice one's chances || *to kill the goose that lays the golden eggs*, to sacrifice everything for the sake of present needs || (*informal*) *the goose hangs high*, everything is going well.

gander *n.* (from Old English *gandra, ganta*) a male goose || (*informal*) *to take a gander*, to have a quick look || (*informal*) a simpleton.

French

canard *n.* (fem. *cane*) duck || (*fig.*) a sugar lump soaked in coffee or alcohol || (*fig.*) inaccurate information in the newspapers || *marcher comme un canard*, to walk like a duck || *être mouillé, trempé comme un canard*, to be drenched to the skin || *il fait un froid de canard*, it is dreadfully cold || *lancer des canards*, to tell trumped up stories || (*informal*) *il n'y a rien à lire dans ce canard*, there is nothing worth reading in this article or newspaper.

oie *n.* (masc. *jars*) goose || (*fig.*) *bête comme une oie*, a silly goose || *une oie blanche*, said of a naïve girl || (*military jargon*) *pas de l'oie*, goosestep.

German

Ente *n.* (derived from Germanic *anata, enita*) duck || (*fig.*) *blaue, fette Ente*, false or unfounded information, used in journalism || *kalte Ente*, a cold punch made with white wine, fruit, slices of lemon and sparkling mineral water || (*fig.*) *schnattern, watscheln wie eine Ente*, to flutter or walk like a goose || (*fig.*) *wie eine bleierne Ente schwimmen*, sink like a stone || (*fig.*) *eine lahme Ente*, slow-coach || (*informal*) *Ente*, the Citroen 2 CV.

Gans *n.* (masc. *Ganser, Ganserich*) (from the German *Gans*, indo-germanic *ghans*) goose || *so eine dumme Gans*, a stupid goose || *eine Gänsehaut bekommen*, to have goose pimples || *Gänsemarsch*, to walk in Indian file || (*fig.*) *Gänsewein*, Adam's ale, water.

Italian

anatra *n.* (from latin *anas*) duck || *camminare come un 'anatra*, to walk like a duck, feet pointing outwards and swaying.

oca *n.* (from late Latin *auca* from an earlier word *avica* derived from *avis*) goose || *far venire, avere la pelle d'oca*, to give someone goose flesh or have goose flesh || *ecco fatto il becco all'oca*, said when a job is finished || *passo dell'oca*, goosestep || (*informal*) *porca l'oca!*, used like an oath || (*fig.*) person, particularly a woman, of low intelligence || *a collo d'oca*, used to describe any object with an S-shaped curve.

papera *n.* gosling or young goose || (*informal*) *fare, prendere una papera* slip of the tongue, error while making a speech || *camminare come una papera*, walk in a comic manner.

Acknowledgements

This book would not have been possible without the contributions of many duck enthusiasts and their collections. The author would like to give particular thanks to the following:

Giorgio Cavallari (psychoanalyst), Carlo Chendi, Tino Ferrari, Franco Fossati, Simonetta Mascagni, Janet Rowlands, Cristiana Scandolara, Margherita Uras, Stefano Vaj, Carlo Violano (ornitholgist) and the shop Pelucherie di Quadriga, Milan.

The excerpt from *The Wild Duck* by Ibsen, translated by Michael Meyer, is reproduced by kind permission of Methuen.

Picture sources

The ducks and geese illustrated in this book belong to the following collections:
Maria Antoncecchi and Illic Feroldi (pp. 10–11);
Pierluigi Caccini (pp. 7, 8, 9, 15, 18, 23, 26, 31, 32, 34, 36, 38–39, 41, 42–43, 47, 48, 51, 53, 54, 57, 58, 59, 62, 65, 66, 69, 73, 75, 86–87, 89, 94, 95, 96, 99, 100);
Lella Costa and Andrea Marietti (pp. 7, 22, 27, 44, 50, 72, 92);
Anna Giorgetti (pp. 70, 83, 85, 90, 97);
Paola Girardi (cover, pp. 7, 16, 21, 25, 29, 40, 45, 66, 81, 84, 91, 98);
Giuliano Monaco (p. 30);
Andriana Pizzocaro (pp. 60–61);
Marco Polillo (pp. 2, 12, 13, 14, 19, 49, 52, 55, 63, 67, 76, 77).

All photographs by Giorgio Coppin in collaboration with Anna Giorgetti.

Illustrations